INHALTSVERZEICHNIS

1 *READING* – LESEÜBUNGEN

My first day at school	5
Maria and Anne	6
Life of a superstar	9
What a disaster!	11
Halloween	12
Unusual animals	14
At a youth camp	16
Explaining the way	18
Lost in Vienna	19
A new friend from outer space	20
Ordering food	23
Families	25
Messages	27
The curse of the mummy	28
An adventure story	30
The best place in my house	32
The weather forecast	34
The weather report	35
Sports	36
At the ghost school	38
My new pet	41
Holidays	43

2 *WRITING* – SCHREIBÜBUNGEN

Last summer	46
Dialogue about holidays	47
A burglary	48
A terrible morning	49

Inhaltsverzeichnis

Halloween	51
Description of a fantasy animal	52
Description of your favourite fantasy animal	54
Explaining the way	55
At a youth camp	57
Party	58
From outer space	59
At a restaurant	61
A ghost story	62
Your house	64
My dream house	66
What a pity!	67
Families	68
Your favourite star	69
The weather	70
The weather forecast for Austria	71
Tomorrow's weather	73
Ancient Egypt	74
Adventure story	75
Sports	76
Linda's favourite sport	77
Paul's favourite sport	78
Pets	79
Dialogue about your pet	80
Animals	81
Rules	82
Schools	83
Your dream school	84
Holidays	85
Plans for next school year	86
How embarrassing!	87

READING – LESEÜBUNGEN

My first day at school

1 Read the text and tick true or false. – *Lies den Text und kreuze richtig oder falsch an.*

It was the first day of my new school year. I couldn't wait to see all my friends again. I had so many exciting stories to tell about my holidays in Greece and about my new dog. Her name is Maya and she is so cute, I love her!
When Mrs Simons, our teacher, came into the room, everyone stood up and said, "Good morning!" Our teacher looked very relaxed and tanned *(sonnengebräunt)*. She smiled at us and said, "Sit down, please! I hope you had a good time and enjoyed your holidays. Who wants to tell me about their holidays?", she asked.
I put my hand up. "Okay, Nicole! Go ahead!"
"My family and I went to Greece in July. We stayed there for two weeks. It was so hot, but luckily *(glücklicherweise)* our apartment was next to the beach and there was air condition in all the rooms".
"So, what did you do in Greece, apart from swimming?", Mrs Simons wanted to know.
"Well, we went to many different places and did some sightseeing, but it was really boring", I answered.
"Did anything exciting happen?", the teacher asked.
"Yes, one day my family and I went to the beach. My little brother, he is only five years old, played in the sand. But suddenly he was gone. Nobody knew where he was. We asked all the people around us and showed them a picture of him. But nobody had seen him *(niemand hatte ihn gesehen)*. My parents were really worried, and my mum almost *(beinahe)* started to cry. Suddenly we saw a man coming towards us. Next to him there was a little boy who was crying. It was my brother! He wanted to buy some ice cream at the snack bar, but he got lost and started to cry."
"Wow, this is a really exciting story, but with a happy ending! Is there anyone else who wants to tell me about their holidays?", Mrs Simons asked. …

		True	False
1	Nicole spent her holidays in Spain.	☐	☐
2	She stayed there for two weeks.	☐	☐
3	The family stayed in a caravan.	☐	☐
4	They stayed close to the beach.	☐	☐
5	Nicole only went swimming.	☐	☐
6	One day something exciting happened.	☐	☐
7	Nicole's brother is three years old.	☐	☐
8	He played in the sand.	☐	☐
9	Nicole's parents called the police.	☐	☐
10	Nicole's brother wanted to buy some ice cream.	☐	☐

1 READING

2 Answer the questions. – *Beantworte die Fragen.*

1 Where did Nicole spend her holidays?
___

2 What is her dog's name?
___

3 What happened when Mrs Simons came into the room?
___

4 What was the weather like in Greece?
___

5 What did Nicole and her family do in Greece?
___

6 Where did they stay?
___

7 Who disappeared *(verschwand)* one day?
___

8 What did the family do then?
___

9 Why did Nicole's brother disappear?
___

10 Was there a happy ending?
___

Maria and Anne

3 Read the texts about Maria and Anne and tick the correct sentences. – *Lies die Texte über Maria und Anne und kreuze die richtigen Sätze an.*

Hi! I'm **Maria**. I am from Lower Austria and I live in a small village. My school is more than an hour from my hometown. I always go there by train. I usually get up at 6 o'clock in the morning, which is really early for me. My train leaves at 7 o'clock and the first lesson starts at half past seven. When the weather is nice, I ride my bike to the station, but when it rains or in winter my mum drives me there.

I usually get home at two o'clock. Then I have lunch with my mum and my granny. In the afternoon, I do my homework. On Mondays and Tuesdays, I go to ballet class. It always starts at half past five and lasts *(dauern)* two hours. I am very good at ballet and I really enjoy it.

Hi! I am **Anne.** I come from England and I live in a small town called Tonbridge, which is an hour from London. So I often go there to do some shopping. You find really great clothes stores there. My favourite one is in Oxford Street.

I haven't got any brothers or sisters, but two cousins. I get on well with them and we do a lot of things together.

We go to the same school. It is a grammar school *(AHS)* for girls only. There is also a grammar school for boys in my town, it is called "The Judd School". My teachers are very strict and there are many rules to keep. We are not allowed to dye our hair *(Haare färben)* or wear make-up. School starts at 9 o'clock. Before the first lesson begins, we all meet in the assembly hall *(Aula)* where our headteacher *(Klassenvorstand)* checks if everyone is here.

The first break is from 10:30 to 11:00, then we have a lunch break at one o'clock, it lasts for an hour. I always have lunch at school because we are not allowed to leave the school grounds *(Schulgelände)*.

I get home at half past four. Then I watch TV, do my homework or play with my dog. When my dad gets home at half past six, we have dinner together. I usually go to bed at 10 o'clock.

1	Maria lives in a small village in Sweden.	☐
2	Her school is about an hour from her hometown.	☐
3	Maria always goes there by bike.	☐
4	She usually has lunch with her mum and her granny.	☐
5	On Mondays and Fridays, she goes to ballet class.	☐
6	Anne comes from England.	☐
7	Her hometown is about two hours from London.	☐
8	Anne often goes shopping in London.	☐
9	Her favourite shoe store is in Carnaby Street.	☐
10	Anne hasn't got any brothers or sisters.	☐
11	She goes to a comprehensive school.	☐
12	Her teachers are very strict.	☐
13	Anne always has lunch at school.	☐
14	After school she does her homework and plays with her friends.	☐

1 READING

4 Write the times. – *Schreibe die Uhrzeiten auf.*

1 Maria's school starts at _____.
2 She usually gets up at _____.
3 Her train leaves at _____.
4 The first lesson starts at _____.
5 Maria usually gets home at _____.
6 Her ballet class starts at _____.
7 Her ballet class ends at _____.
8 Anne's school starts at _____.
9 The first break is from _____ to _____.
10 Lunch break starts at _____.
11 Lunch break ends at _____.
12 Anne gets home at _____.
13 Her dad gets home at _____.
14 Anne usually goes to bed at _____.

Life of a superstar

5 Read the text about the famous British singer Adele. Then answer the questions. – *Lies den Text über die berühmte britische Sängerin Adele. Dann beantworte die Fragen.*

Adele was born in London on May 5th, 1988. Her full name is Adele Laurie Blue Adkins. Her parents got divorced when she was only two years old. Adele began singing at the age of four.

In 1997, the singer and her mum moved *(umziehen)* to Brighton. In 1999, they moved back to London where Adele went to the BRIT School for Performing Arts and Technology.

Adele's son Angelo was born on October 19th, 2012. In April 2019, Adele and her husband, Simon Konecki, separated *(sich trennen)*.

Adele's most famous songs are "Hello", "Rolling in the Deep" and "Skyfall". She is one of the most popular singers in the world.

1 Where was Adele born?

2 When is her birthday?

3 What is her full name?

4 When did her parents divorce?

5 At what age did Adele start singing?

6 Where did Adele and her mum move to in 1997?

7 When was Adele's son born?

8 What is his name?

9 What is Adele's husband's name?

10 What are her most famous songs?

1 READING

6 Complete the interview with words from the text. – *Vervollständige das Interview mit Wörtern aus dem Text.*

Reporter: Welcome to the studio, Adele! How are you today?

Adele: I am fine, thanks.

Reporter: Great! Can you tell us about your life and childhood *(Kindheit)*?

Adele: Of course! My full name is _____ and I was born in _____ on _____.

Reporter: What can you tell us about your parents?

Adele: My mum and dad _____ when I was only _____ years old. In 1997, my mum and I moved to _____, where I spent the following two years. Then we moved back to _____.

Reporter: Can you tell us when you started singing?

Adele: Yes, I started at _____. I have always enjoyed singing. This is the reason why I went to the _____, where I also graduated *(einen Abschluss machen)*.

Reporter: What is your son's name and how old is he now?

Adele: His name is _____ and he was born on _____, so he is almost seven. I love him and I am so proud of him.

Reporter: Is it true that you and your husband _____ a few months ago?

Adele: Unfortunately *(unglücklicherweise)* it's true, but we are still friends.

Reporter: Thank you very much for the interview and all the best for the future!

I started singing at the age of four, too. But I'm not so famous as Adele.

What a disaster!

7 Read the text and tick true or false. – *Lies den Text und kreuze richtig oder falsch an.*

Last month I was invited to my cousin's birthday party, but I lost the invitation, so I forgot that it was a fancy-dress party. I put on my new skirt with an elegant blouse and my black ballerinas. When I looked at myself in the mirror, I thought, "Wow, you look really pretty!" Then I took my bag and the present for my cousin.

Usually it takes me about 20 minutes by bus to get to her place, but there was a traffic jam and I arrived 30 minutes late.

Quickly I ran to her house. I could already hear loud music and people laughing. Obviously *(offensichtlich)*, the party was great fun. When I rang the doorbell, I heard steps coming towards the door. Someone opened. It was a girl who looked like an alien from outer space. She had green hair and a mask and she wore a really strange costume. First, I did not even recognise her, but then the girl said "Hi Linda! Come in! But where is your costume? Have you got it in your bag?" It was my cousin! I felt so embarrassed! "Uhm, I'm sorry", I stuttered *(stotterte)*, "but I forgot that it is a fancy-dress party. I haven't got a costume with me." Then my cousin started to laugh. "Don't worry", she said, "I'm sure we can find something for you."

In the end I had a lot of fun, but I hope that next time I will not lose the invitation.

		True	False
1	Linda was invited to her friend's birthday party.	☐	☐
2	She lost the invitation.	☐	☐
3	Linda put on jeans and an elegant blouse.	☐	☐
4	Usually it takes her about 20 minutes to get there.	☐	☐
5	Linda was too late because she missed the bus.	☐	☐
6	A girl who looked like a witch opened the door.	☐	☐
7	She had black hair and wore a mask.	☐	☐
8	Linda felt so embarrassed.	☐	☐
9	Her cousin didn't have a costume for Linda.	☐	☐
10	In the end Linda had a lot of fun.	☐	☐

READING

8 Complete the dialogue with the words from the text. – *Vervollständige den Dialog mit Wörtern aus dem Text.*

M: Hi Linda! How was the party? Did you have a good time?

L: Oh Mum! It was so _____.

M: Why? What happened, my dear?

L: Well, you know that I put on my new _____, an elegant _____ and _____ ballerinas?

M: Yes, of course! You looked pretty. Was anything wrong with your outfit?

L: The problem was that I lost the _____, so I did not remember that it was a _____.

M: Oh no! How embarrassing! What did you do then?

L: Thank God, Louisa lent *(borgte)* me one of her _____.

M: I understand. So, did you enjoy the party then?

L: Yes, in the end it was great fun and I met this good-looking guy …

Halloween

9 Read the text and combine the sentence halves. – *Lies den Text und verbinde die passenden Satzteile miteinander.*

Peter was so sad. It was Halloween and he couldn't go trick-or-treating with his friends because he was ill. No sweets, no scary costumes – nothing!

His mum tried to cheer him up *(aufheitern)* and baked one of his favourite cakes, but Peter was not hungry.

At least *(zumindest)* he could watch TV, and so he decided to watch a horror movie. It was completely dark outside, and the wind was blowing. On the screen a monster appeared and attacked a girl who screamed loudly. Peter felt a little scared. Suddenly he heard a knock at his bedroom window. First, he thought that it was just the wind, but then he heard it again. He turned down the volume and almost forgot to breathe *(atmen)*. There it was again, this time even louder. Peter didn't know what to do. He hid under his blanket *(Decke)* and hoped that the noise would stop, but it didn't.

Finally, he decided to get up and have a look. Slowly, he went to the window and looked outside. And what did he see?

His best friends stood there, they laughed and shouted, "Trick or Treat"!

Peter also laughed, opened the window and said, "Come in! I'm sure my mum has got some sweets for you!"

It was Halloween and	1	A	and baked one of his favourite cakes.
It was completely dark outside	2	B	it was just the wind, but then he heard it again.
His mum tried to cheer him up	3	C	and the wind was blowing.
At least he could watch TV,	4	D	and hoped that the noise would stop.
On the screen a monster appeared	5	E	opened the window and said, "Come in!"
He turned down the volume	6	F	and almost forgot to breathe.
First, he thought that	7	G	and so he decided to watch a horror film.
He hid under his blanket	8	H	to get up and have a look.
Finally, he decided	9	I	and attacked a girl who screamed loudly.
His best friends stood there,	10	J	Peter couldn't go trick or treating with his friends.
Peter laughed,	11	K	laughed and shouted, "Trick or Treat"!

10 Answer the questions. – *Beantworte die Fragen.*

1 Why was Peter sad?
___

2 What did his mum try to do?
___

3 What did Peter watch?
___

4 What did Peter suddenly hear?
___

5 How did he feel?
___

6 Did the noise stop?
___

7 Did Peter get up?
___

8 Who did he see when he looked out of the window?
___

Unusual animals

11 Read the text about unusual animals that lived in the lost city of Atlantis and tick true or false. – *Lies den Text über ungewöhnliche Tiere, die in der verlorenen Stadt von Atlantis lebten, und kreuze richtig oder falsch an.*

The gigantic peacock
The gigantic peacock was as big as an elephant, but it was not dangerous. It was very heavy, so it could not fly. It was a very friendly animal and only ate flowers and plants.

The tiny octopus
The tiny octopus was as small as a fly, but very dangerous. Its poison could kill many other animals. It could swim really fast. Its tentacles were blue and green. Many people were afraid of it.

The ugly dog
The ugly dog was a kind of dragon. Its head looked like a dog's head, but its body looked like a dragon. It could fly really fast and only ate mice. It was a very friendly animal and many people had an ugly dog as a pet.

		True	False
1	The tiny octopus was very dangerous.	☐	☐
2	The gigantic peacock was a very friendly animal.	☐	☐
3	Many people were afraid of the ugly dog.	☐	☐
4	The gigantic peacock was very heavy.	☐	☐
5	The gigantic peacock could fly really fast.	☐	☐
6	The tiny octopus was bigger than a fly.	☐	☐
7	The ugly dog only ate mice.	☐	☐
8	The ugly dog was a very unfriendly animal.	☐	☐
9	People kept ugly dogs in their homes.	☐	☐
10	The gigantic peacock only ate flowers and insects.	☐	☐
11	The tiny octopus's tentacles were blue and green.	☐	☐
12	The ugly dog's body looked like a dragon.	☐	☐
13	The gigantic peacock was bigger than an elephant.	☐	☐
14	The gigantic peacock only ate flowers and plants.	☐	☐
15	Nobody was afraid of the tiny octopus.	☐	☐

12 Answer the questions. – *Beantworte die Fragen.*

1 How big was the gigantic peacock?
_____

2 Why was its poison so dangerous?
_____

3 Could the gigantic peacock fly?
_____

4 What did the gigantic peacock eat?
_____

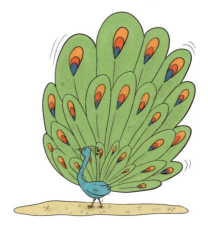

5 How big was the tiny octopus?
_____

6 Why was the tiny octopus so dangerous?
_____

7 What was the tiny octopus really good at?
_____

8 How did his tentacles look like?
_____

9 What did the ugly dog look like?
_____

10 What did the ugly dog eat?
_____

11 What was the ugly dog really good at?
_____

12 Did people like the ugly dog?
_____

At a youth camp

13 Read the text and tick the correct sentences. – *Lies den Text und kreuze die richtigen Sätze an.*

Hi Mum and Dad,

The camp is fantastic! I'm so happy to be here. Every day we do so many interesting things. On the first day we went rock climbing. At first, I was a bit scared, but then I couldn't stop. My teacher said, "You are the best climber in the world!" I felt so proud.

On Tuesday we went rafting. It was really exciting, but I fell into the water and hurt my ankle *(Knöchel)*. And the water was freezing cold *(eiskalt)*. So I don't think I will do it again.

Today we went swimming in the lake. I had so much fun. We played water ball and my team won.

Tomorrow might be a bit boring, because we are going to visit a castle. You know, I'm not really into knights *(Ritter)* and stuff *(hier: Kram, Zeug)* like that.

The only thing I don't like is the food here. We never get pizza or lasagne, only healthy stuff like salads and vegetables.

I hope you are well and have a good time.

See you soon!

Love,
Paul

1	Paul enjoys the camp.	☐
2	They don't do many interesting things.	☐
3	On the first day, he went rock climbing.	☐
4	He wasn't good at it.	☐
5	On Tuesday, they went swimming.	☐
6	On Tuesday, Paul hurt his ankle.	☐
7	Paul played water ball but his team lost.	☐
8	Paul doesn't like castles.	☐
9	Paul doesn't like the food there.	☐
10	They always get pizza and lasagne.	☐

14 Answer the questions. – *Beantworte die Fragen.*

1 What did Paul do on the first day?
_____

2 Was he good at climbing?
_____

3 What did Paul do on Tuesday?
_____

4 Why doesn't he want to go rafting again?
_____

5 Who won the water ball competition?
_____

6 Why doesn't Paul want to visit the castle?
_____

7 Why doesn't he like the food there?
_____

Explaining the way

15 Read Tommy's email and draw the route on the map. – *Lies Tommys E-Mail und zeichne seinen Weg in der Karte ein.*

Dear Tony,

I'm glad that you can come to my birthday party next week. I'm not sure if you know the way to my house, so I am going to describe it to you.

You said that you would come by train, right? When you leave the station, you first have to turn right and walk down Burger Street. Go past the post office and then cross the bridge. After the bridge there is a roundabout *(Kreisverkehr)*, take the second exit and go down Lansbury Road. There is also a supermarket on the left. At the end of the street, turn right into Kanastian Road. My house is the third on the left, number 3. It is white, with a green roof. You can't miss it!

If you get lost, please call me at 006-48732.

See you next week!
Cheers, Tommy

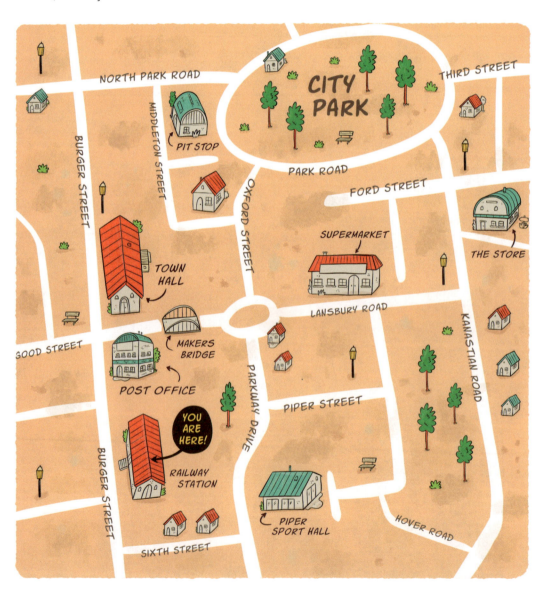

Lost in Vienna

16 Read the text and fill in the missing words. – *Lies den Text und setze die fehlenden Wörter ein.*

Barbara and Julie are in Vienna. They come from New York and they are visiting their grandparents. They are staying for one week.
One day they want to go sightseeing in the first district *(1. Bezirk)*, but on their way to the underground station they get lost. So they ask some people for help.

Barbara: Excuse me, can you tell me the way to the underground station?
Man 1: Which one do you mean?
Barbara: I think, the one next to the opera house.
Man 1: Oh, I see, that's easy. First, go past the cinema and turn left. Then turn into Siebenbrunnengasse, there is a small supermarket on the left-hand side. After about 200 metres, turn right and just go straight ahead. After a few minutes you can already see the opera house and there is the underground station.
Barbara: Thank you, sir!
Man 1: You're welcome!

(Ten minutes later)
Julie: I think we got lost again. There is no opera house and I didn't see any supermarket either *(auch nicht)*.
Barbara: I think you are right. Let's ask that woman over there.
Julie: Excuse me, can you tell me how to get to the underground station?
Woman: I'm sorry, I'm not from here.
Julie: What shall we do now?
Barbara: Let's take a taxi!

1 Barbara and Julie _____ from New York.
2 They are visiting their _____.
3 They _____ for _____ week.
4 On the way to the underground _____ they _____ lost.
5 A man tells them that it is _____ to get to the opera house.
6 He says that they first must go past the _____ and turn _____ there.
7 The man explains that there is a small _____ on the _____ side.
8 Julie thinks that they got _____ again.
9 Barbara asks a _____.
10 The woman _____ from Vienna   .
11 Barbara decides to _____ a taxi.

A new friend from outer space

17 Read the text, then put the pictures on page 21 into the correct order. – *Lies den Text und bringe dann die 10 Bilder von Seite 21 in die richtige Reihenfolge.*

It was a sunny day when Mrs Miller was walking her dog Jerry. Usually Jerry did not go far away because he was a bit shy and so always stayed close to his owner *(Besitzer)*. But when they arrived at the park, Jerry suddenly started to bark loudly and ran behind the bushes. "Jerry! Come back!", Mrs Miller shouted. But the dog didn't listen. The woman became angry and went after the dog. "Jerry, where are you?", she shouted. Then she heard a noise. Slowly she went towards the bushes, and there she saw a small green creature. It had a big head with large eyes and a small mouth. On its head there were black antennas *(Fühler)*. Its arms were as long as a spider's legs and its legs were very short. It looked really strange. Mrs Miller panicked and started to shout for help. But suddenly the strange creature smiled and calmly *(ruhig)* said to her, "Don't be afraid! I am Spocki, and I come from Planet Venus. I cannot find my spaceship. But I am not dangerous. Could you please help me?"

"Hmmm, well, I don't know if I can," Mrs Miller stuttered *(stotterte)*.

"Could you lend me your mobile phone?", Spocki asked.

"What do you need it for?", the woman wanted to know. "So that I can phone my friends and they can tell me where they are," the alien explained.

Slowly Mrs Miller gave it her mobile phone. Spocki quickly took it, dialed a number and said something in a strange language. Then it looked at the woman and smiled. "Thank you!", it said. It went off and suddenly disappeared. Mrs Miller still couldn't believe what she had just seen *(sie gerade gesehen hatte)*.

18 Tick true or false. – *Kreuze richtig oder falsch an.*

		True	False
1	It was a rainy day when Mrs Miller was walking her dog Jerry.	☐	☐
2	Jerry always stayed close to his owner.	☐	☐
3	The dog didn't listen to Mrs Miller.	☐	☐
4	Mrs Miller saw a strange light.	☐	☐
5	She saw a small creature with a big head.	☐	☐
6	Mrs Miller panicked and ran off.	☐	☐
7	The strange creature smiled.	☐	☐
8	It is called Spocki and comes from Planet Utopia.	☐	☐
9	Spocki asked Mrs Miller for her mobile phone.	☐	☐
10	Mrs Miller didn't give it her mobile phone.	☐	☐
11	Spocki said something in a strange language.	☐	☐
12	It suddenly disappeared.	☐	☐

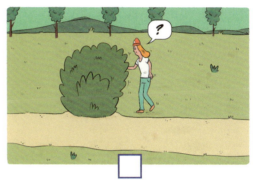
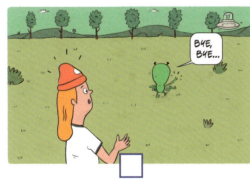

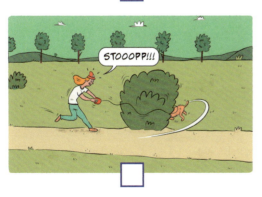

1 READING

19 Complete the interview with words from the text. – *Vervollständige das Interview mit Wörtern aus dem Text.*

Interviewer: Welcome to the news on FF1! Today our guest is Mrs Miller from Canterbury.
Last week she met an alien and now she is going to tell us about this exciting experience.
Good evening, Mrs Miller. Thank you for coming!

Mrs M: Good evening!

Interviewer: Could you please tell us what happened last Monday!

Mrs M: Yes, of course. It was a _____ day and I _____ my dog Jerry in the park. Usually Jerry is rather shy and he always stays _____ to me, but last Monday everything was different.

Interviewer: What happened?

Mrs M: Jerry ran behind the _____ and did not come back. So, I decided to follow him.

Interviewer: Why didn't he come back?

Mrs M: At first I didn't know, but then I suddenly saw a strange creature. I was so shocked!

Interviewer: Can you describe it?

Mrs M: Yes, of course. It had a _____ head and a large _____. On its head there were black _____.

Interviewer: What did you do then?

Mrs M: At first I shouted for _____, but then the creature spoke to me and I realised *(erkannte)* that it was not dangerous.

Interviewer: Did it tell you its name and where it came from?

Mrs M: Yes, it did. Its name was _____ and it came from _____.

Interviewer: Did it say anything else?

Mrs M: It wanted to borrow my _____, because it needed to phone its friends. I gave it my phone and then it went off.

Interviewer: This was a really exciting story, Mrs Miller. Thank you for the interview!

Mrs M: You are welcome.

Ordering food

20 Read the dialogue and answer the questions on the next side. – *Lies den Text und beantworte die Fragen auf der nächsten Seite.*

Waiter: A table for two?

Mr Potter: No, we need a table for three, our daughter's bus is delayed *(verspätet)*, so she is coming a bit later.

Waiter: Okay. Next to the window, sir?

Mrs Potter: That's fine.

Mr Potter: Could we have the menu, please?

Waiter: Of course! Can I get you something to drink?

Mrs Potter: For me, a glass of diet coke, please.

Waiter: And for you, sir?

Mr Potter: Mineral water, please.

(Five minutes later)

Mrs Potter: Hi Jenny! We are sitting over here, next to the window!

Mr Potter: Hello my dear! I'm glad that you finally made it. Everything okay? You look so tired.

Jenny: Hi Mum and Dad! It was a hard day and I am starving *(ich verhungere)*. Do you already know what you're going to order?

Mrs Potter: Well, I'll take the pizza with salami and cheese. My friends at work said that they have the best pizzas in town here.

Mr Potter: I'm not sure. I think I'll take the fish with potatoes and vegetables. And what about you, Jenny?

Jenny: Well, I'll take the tomato soup.

Mrs Potter: Only tomato soup? Aren't you hungry?

Jenny: It is the only vegetarian dish on the menu. Did I forget to tell you that I don't eat meat anymore?

Badges eat everything!
(Dachse sind Allesfresser!)

1 Why does Jenny come late?

2 Where is their table?

3 What does Mrs Potter order to drink?

4 What does Mr Potter order to drink?

5 Why does Jenny look tired?

6 Is she hungry?

7 What does Mrs Potter want to eat?

8 Who said that they had the best pizzas in town there?

9 What does Mr Potter want to eat?

10 Why does Jenny only order tomato soup?

That's my menu!

Families

21 Read the texts about different families and tick the correct sentences. – *Lies die Texte über verschiedene Familien und kreuze die richtigen Sätze an.*

I'm **Jacob** and I'm from **Austria**. I live in a small town called Neustadt. Our house is not very big, but it has a beautiful garden with a nice swimming pool. In summer my friends and I spend the whole day there. I've got two older brothers. Michael is 16 years old and David is 20. David moved out a year ago. He lives in a flat in Vienna, Sometimes I visit him there. My brother Michael is my best friend. We do a lot of things together and sometimes he takes me on a ride on his motorbike.

I'm **Soko** and I live in **Japan**. I don't have any brothers or sisters. My parents both work the whole day and often I feel bored. Then I invite my friends and we do our homework together or we go to the cinema or shopping centre.
I live in a small flat, but I have my own room. This is really great. I need my privacy. The rest of my family lives far away, so I don't see them very often.

I am **Carla**. I come from **Spain**. I live in Madrid, the capital of Spain. I love this city because there are so many interesting things to do there. My parents have a big house. I like our garden best with all the beautiful flowers and orange trees.
I have got a sister. She is four years old and her name is Sofia. Sometimes she gets on my nerves, but most of the time I get on well with her.
My grandparents live in the same street, so I see them almost every day. My mum only works part-time *(Teilzeit)* and my dad is an architect. He usually comes home late in the evening and sometimes he has to work on weekends, too.

1	Jacob lives in Neustadt.	☐
2	His house is not very big.	☐
3	In summer he spends the whole day at the swimming pool.	☐
4	His brother Michael moved out a year ago.	☐
5	His brother David lives in a flat in Vienna.	☐
6	Soko hasn't got any brothers or sisters.	☐
7	Soko's mum doesn't work.	☐
8	Soko lives in a small flat.	☐
9	Soko's dad works the whole day.	☐
10	Carla doesn't like Madrid.	☐
11	Carla likes her room best.	☐
12	She has got a younger sister.	☐
13	Most of the time she gets on well with her.	☐
14	Carla's grandparents live far away from her.	☐
15	Carla's dad is a dentist.	☐
16	Her mum only works part-time.	☐

22 Who says what? Write Jacob, Soko or Carla next to the sentences. – *Wer sagt was? Schreibe Jacob, Soko oder Carla neben die Sätze.*

1 My parents work the whole day. _____
2 I like our garden best. _____
3 His brother lives in Vienna. _____
4 I have my own room. This is really important to me. _____
5 I live in a small town called Neustadt. _____
6 My mum works part-time. _____
7 I need my privacy. _____
8 My sister's name is Sofia. _____
9 I don't have any brothers or sisters. _____
10 The rest of my family lives far away. _____
11 My dad usually comes home late in the evening. _____
12 My grandparents live in the same street. _____
13 I love Madrid. _____
14 I live in Japan. _____
15 I'm from Austria. _____

Messages

23 Read the messages and tick the correct answers. – *Lies die Nachrichten und kreuze die richtigen Antworten an.*

Hi Robert! Thanks for inviting me to your party next Saturday! I'm not sure if I can come because I might have to go to my granny's birthday party. I'll ask Mum if I can come to your party, but I'm not sure what she will answer.
I'll let you know! See you! Richard

Richard, no problem. I can understand that your granny's birthday is more important than my party. Of course, it would be great if you could come. But we can also meet up another time.

Hey! Guess what! Granny fell ill and so she is going to celebrate her birthday one week later. That means I can come to your party! I have got a big surprise for you. I can't wait to see your face when you open my present! See you! Richard

Richard! I'm so sorry to tell you that my party is going to take place one week later, too. My grandpa is in hospital and we are going to visit him at the weekend. He lives two hours away, so Mum says that I can't have my party this Saturday. Sorry! Robert

1 What does Richard say in his message to Robert?

A	He is going to visit his cousin.	☐
B	He might go to his granny's birthday party.	☐
C	He can't come.	☐

2 What does Robert write in his first message?

A	They can also meet up another time.	☐
B	They can go to the cinema.	☐
C	They can go to a football match.	☐

3 What does Robert write in his answer?

A	His granny is going to celebrate her birthday one week later.	☐
B	His granny is going to be on holiday.	☐
C	His granny is not going to celebrate her birthday at all.	☐

4 What does Robert say in his last message?

A	His mum is in hospital.	☐
B	He is ill.	☐
C	His grandpa is in hospital.	☐

The curse of the mummy

24 Read the text and underline the five wrong sentences. – *Lies den Text und unterstreiche die vier falschen Sätze.*

Hannah and Patrick went to Egypt with their parents. Both were really excited, because they had never been so far away *(waren noch nie so weit weg gewesen)*.

Their first stop was Cairo, where they wanted to go sightseeing. They went to the cinema. After a few days they wanted to go to the Red Sea to relax at the beach.

On their first day in Cairo, Hannah, Patrick and their parents went to the Egyptian Museum. Patrick didn't like his new shoes. There the guide told them an interesting story about the mummy of a Queen who had been the most beautiful woman ever, even more beautiful than Queen Cleopatra. "Can we see the mummy?" Hannah asked the man. "I'm sorry, young lady, but a few days ago the mummy suddenly disappeared. We informed the police, but they haven't found anything. There are no signs of a burglary *(keine Einbruchsspuren)*. The ambulance arrived. It is very mysterious", the guide explained. He looked a bit frightened.

"Oh, this is a really interesting story. Let's hope you will find the mummy soon", their dad said.

When the family left the museum, they decided to go back to their hotel to relax. Hannah and Patrick stayed in the lobby because they were not tired.

Suddenly Hannah said, "Let's go back to the museum and try to find the mummy!" "I don't know if this is a good idea!" Patrick answered. "Don't be such a coward *(Feigling)*! Come on, we'll be back in an hour and Mum and Dad will not even know we were gone." She stood up and left the lobby. Her brother followed her and bought a new pair of jeans.

When they arrived at the museum, they went to the room with all the mummies. There was one empty space. "Here it is", Hannah whispered *(flüsterte)*. No one else was in the room. Suddenly Patrick said, "Look, there is a small door over there! Let's find out what is behind it." Quickly he opened the door and went in. His sister followed him. It was completely dark and the children couldn't see anything, but then Patrick turned on the flashlight on his mobile phone. They were in a small room and at the end they could see some light. Hannah quickly went there, but Patrick was too scared to move. Then he heard a terrible scream …

25 Tick true or false. – *Kreuze richtig oder falsch an.*

	True	False
1 It was the first time Hannah and Patrick went so far away.	☐	☐
2 Their first stop was the Red Sea.	☐	☐
3 On their first day in Cairo, they went to the Egyptian Museum.	☐	☐
4 The guide told them an interesting story about the pyramids.	☐	☐
5 A few years ago a mummy had suddenly disappeared.	☐	☐
6 There were no signs of a burglary.	☐	☐
7 Hannah and Patrick stayed in their rooms.	☐	☐
8 They went to the room with all the mummies.	☐	☐
9 No one else was in the room.	☐	☐
10 Hannah opened the small door.	☐	☐
11 Patrick turned on the flashlight on his mobile phone.	☐	☐
12 They were in a big room.	☐	☐
13 There was a bright light.	☐	☐
14 Hannah was too scared to move.	☐	☐
15 Patrick heard a terrible scream.	☐	☐

26 Put the sentences into the correct order – *Bringe die Sätze in die richtige Reihenfolge*

☐ On their first day in Cairo, Hannah, Patrick and their parents went to the Egyptian Museum.

☐ When they arrived at the museum, they went to the room with all the mummies.

☐ There the guide told them an interesting story about the mummy of a queen who had been the most beautiful woman ever,

☐ His sister followed him. It was completely dark and the children couldn't see anything.

☐ When the family left the museum, they decided to go back to their hotel to relax.

☐ Their first stop was Cairo, where they wanted to go sightseeing.

☐ Hannah and Patrick went to Egypt with their parents.

☐ We immediately informed the police, but they haven't found anything. There are no signs of a burglary.

☐ Hannah and Patrick stayed in the lobby because they were not tired.

☐ They were in a small room and at its end they could see some light.

READING

An adventure story

27 Read the story and put the pictures on page 31 in order. – *Lies die Geschichte und bringe die Bilder auf Seite 31 in die richtige Reihenfolge.*

Last summer my family and I went camping. It was my first camping holiday and I was really excited. My parents wanted to go to a nearby wood. We got up early in the morning, because we wanted to be there as soon as possible. It was a beautiful day. The sun was shining brightly and it was really warm.

When we got there, we put up our tents. There was a river close-by, and we spent the whole day there. We had so much fun! When it got dark, we made a fire and told each other scary ghost stories. My mum was afraid that we would have nightmares *(Albträume)*. But I wasn't scared at all.

It was almost midnight when we finally lay down in our tents. I shared mine *(ich teilte meines)* with my younger brother Paul.

Suddenly I heard a noise, then a scream. It was Paul. "There is someone outside! It's a wolf and it is going to eat us!", he shouted. "Don't be silly!", I answered. "There are no wolves in this forest." I took my torch and slowly went outside.

At first, I couldn't see anything, but then I noticed a small animal. It was a hedgehog *(Igel)*. I started to laugh.

28 Tick true or false. – *Kreuze richtig oder falsch an.*

		True	False
1	Last summer my friends and I went camping.	☐	☐
2	My parents wanted to go to a nearby wood.	☐	☐
3	It was a beautiful day.	☐	☐
4	There was a lake close-by.	☐	☐
5	We told each other scary ghost stories.	☐	☐
6	I shared my tent with my younger sister.	☐	☐
7	Paul thought there was a wolf outside.	☐	☐
8	I called my parents.	☐	☐
9	I could see a shadow.	☐	☐
10	It was a hedgehog.	☐	☐

The best place in my house

29 Who says what? Write Anna, Peter, Caroline or Jacob next to the sentences. – *Wer sagt was? Schreibe Anna, Peter, Caroline oder Jacob neben die Sätze.*

Anna: The best place in my house is the bathroom. I have got my own bathroom. It is not very big, but it has everything I need: a sink *(Waschbecken)*, a shower and, most important, a makeup stand *(Schminktisch)* with a big mirror. The tiles *(Fliesen)* are white with blue flowers and the floor is grey. I like my bathroom because there I can relax and enjoy my privacy.

Peter: The best place in my house is the garage. In it there are my bike, my dad's car – a sports car – and many tools. I love repairing things and I often help my dad fix *(reparieren)* something in the house. Our garage is really big and there are two windows that overlook the garden. I like this place best because I feel like a man there.

Caroline: The best place in my house is the living room. It is not very big, but cosy *(gemütlich)*. The sofa is very comfortable and there is a big flat screen TV on the wall. I like the pot plants and white curtains. There are also a big bookshelf and a small desk. I like this place best because I feel comfortable there.

Jacob: The best place in my house is the kitchen. There is a big table with eight chairs where we always have lunch and dinner. There is also a small table with two chairs where we have breakfast on school days. There are a sink, a dishwasher, a cooker *(Herd)* and a big fridge. Our kitchen is new and very modern.
I like the kitchen best because it is a place where it always smells good.

1. I love repairing things. _____
2. There is a big table with eight chairs. _____
3. The tiles are white with blue flowers. _____
4. The sofa is very comfortable. _____
5. Our kitchen is new. _____
6. Our garage is big and there are two windows that overlook the garden. _____
7. I like this place best because I feel like a man there. _____
8. The sofa is very comfortable. _____
9. It is a place where it always smells good. _____
10. There is also a big bookshelf. _____
11. There are a sink, a dishwasher and a cooker. _____
12. I like the pot plants and white curtains. _____
13. There is also a small table with two chairs. _____
14. It is not very big, but cosy. _____
15. I can relax and enjoy my privacy. _____

30 Tick the correct sentences. – *Kreuze die richtigen Sätze an.*

1 The tiles in Anna's bathroom are grey.	☐
2 Anna's bathroom is not very big.	☐
3 There are a sink, a shower and a small mirror in it.	☐
4 Peter loves repairing things and he often helps his dad.	☐
5 There is no bike in the garage.	☐
6 There are two windows that overlook the garden.	☐
7 Caroline's living room is not very big, but cosy.	☐
8 Caroline doesn't like the white curtains.	☐
9 Jacob's favourite place is the kitchen.	☐
10 There is a big table with five chairs.	☐
11 The kitchen is a place where it always smells good.	☐
12 There are a sink and a fridge, but not a dishwasher.	☐

My best place is the skatepark!

READING

The weather forecast

31 Put the dialogues into the correct order. – *Bringe die Dialoge in die richtige Reihenfolge.*

Dialogue 1:

☐ *Josh:* Let me check my mobile phone. You're right, the weather is going to be fine all day.

☐ *Robert:* Nice day today. Let's go swimming.

☐ *Josh:* On TV they said there might be thunderstorms in the afternoon.

☐ *Robert:* Let's go then.

☐ *Josh:* Yes, good idea! But maybe we should go tomorrow.

☐ *Robert:* Are you sure? There are no clouds.

☐ *Robert:* Why?

(3 hours later)

☐ *Robert:* And the wind is really strong.

☐ *Josh:* On no! Look at those clouds over there!

☐ *Josh:* Hurry up or we'll get wet.

☐ *Robert:* You were right. Next time we should listen to the weather forecast on TV.

☐ *Josh:* I think we'd better go home.

Dialogue 2:

☐ *Paul:* Dad, can you turn up the volume, please? I want to listen to the weather report.

☐ *Mum:* Come on! Get in the car! We want to go!

☐ *Weatherman:* … In the east of Austria showers will be quite heavy and there is a high risk of thunderstorms, especially in the mountains. Temperatures will drop to eight degrees during the day.

☐ *Dad:* It's such a nice day, I'm really looking forward to the hiking tour.

☐ *Paul:* Great! And then we could also go to the new burger place. All my friends say they have the best cheeseburgers in the world!

☐ *Mum:* I'm not sure anymore. Maybe we'd better stay at home and go next week.

☐ *Dad:* You're right. But I've got an idea … Let's go to the new shopping centre in town! I need some hiking boots.

☐ *Paul:* Do you really think we should go hiking?

The weather report

32 Read the text and tick true or false. – *Lies den Text und kreuze richtig oder falsch an.*

Good evening, ladies and gentlemen, this is the weather forecast for tomorrow and next week.
In the south, the nice weather will continue with lots of sunshine. There might only be some thunderstorms in the evenings. Temperatures will rise to 35 degrees, so it's perfect weather for swimming. There is a light wind coming up.
In the north, we expect lots of rain. Strong winds are coming up and temperatures will drop to 15 degrees. So don't forget your jumpers *(Pullover)*!

Now the outlook for the rest of the week. Looking at the weather map, we can see that the sunny and warm weather continues in the south with mild temperatures in the morning. There will be long periods of sunshine.
In the north, it will clear up *(aufklaren)* during the day and there will even be sunny spells in the afternoon. Temperatures will rise to 22 degrees.

		True	False
1	In the south there will be lots of rain tomorrow.	☐	☐
2	There might be thunderstorms in the evenings.	☐	☐
3	In the south, temperatures will rise to 32 degrees.	☐	☐
4	In the north, there will be lots of rain tomorrow.	☐	☐
5	Temperatures will drop to 10 degrees in the north.	☐	☐
6	For the rest of the week the sunny and warm weather will continue in the north.	☐	☐
7	In the north, the weather will not get better.	☐	☐
8	In the north, temperatures will rise to 22 degrees.	☐	☐

Sports

33 Read the email and answer the questions. – *Lies die E-Mail und beantworte die Fragen.*

Hi Laura,

Guess what! I had my first riding lesson yesterday. It was fantastic. At first, I was a bit nervous, but after a few minutes I calmed down. My horse is called Usambra. She is a Friesian *(Friese)*, the biggest horse I have ever seen. But she is really cute. My riding instructor *(Reitlehrer)* is called Verena. She is very friendly and also patient *(geduldig)*. Verena is an excellent rider. She has got two horses; one is called Jacky and the other one is Shaba.

Tomorrow I am going to buy new trousers, a helmet and boots. Mum says that I have to pay for the riding lessons myself, because they are very expensive, and I get enough pocket money. Maybe I can sometimes babysit my neighbour's daughter. She is only three years old, so that I can earn some extra money.

I ride twice a week, on Mondays and Fridays. Luckily, the riding stable is close to where I live. It only takes me ten minutes by bike to get there. In the holidays I want to go there every day and help feed and groom *(striegeln)* the horses.

See you soon!

Nora

1 When did Nora have her first riding lesson?

2 Was she nervous at the beginning?

3 What's her horse's name?

4 What's her riding instructor's name?

5 Is she very patient?

6 How many horses has she got?

7 What are their names?

8 Who has to pay for the riding lessons?

9 What does Nora want to do to earn some extra money?
_____

10 How often does she ride?
_____

11 How long does it take her to get to the stable?
_____

12 What does she want to do in her holidays?
_____

34 Tick true or false. – *Kreuze richtig oder falsch an.*

		True	False
1	Nora wasn't nervous at the beginning.	☐	☐
2	Nora's horse is called Usambra.	☐	☐
3	Her riding instructor is called Catherine.	☐	☐
4	Verena is an excellent rider.	☐	☐
5	Verena's horses are called Jacky and Nancy.	☐	☐
6	Nora must pay for the riding lessons herself.	☐	☐
7	Nora wants to look after her cousin.	☐	☐
8	Nora rides twice a week.	☐	☐
9	It only takes her three minutes by bike to get to the stable.	☐	☐
10	In the holidays Nora wants to go to the stable every day.	☐	☐

At the ghost school

35 Read the story and underline the five wrong sentences. – *Lies die Geschichte und unterstreiche die fünf falschen Sätze.*

I am a ghost teacher. Today was my first day at the new school. It is an old castle high up on a mountain. I walked my dog. Luckily, I can fly, so I didn't have to walk or take the train.

When I arrived at the castle, I knocked at the heavy door. I heard steps. Someone opened. A gigantic creature with two heads appeared *(erschien)*. I stepped back, because this was the most terrifying monster I had ever seen *(ich je gesehen hatte)*. "What do you want?" it asked. "I am Haunty, the new teacher", I stuttered *(stotterte)*. I had a cup of tea. "Follow me!" the creature said. We passed through a big hall with pictures of many different ghosts and monsters on the wall. Some of them smiled at me and waved, others just looked really threatening *(bedrohlich)*. Then we went upstairs and finally came to a long corridor. There were spiderwebs everywhere. Thank God. I'm not afraid of spiders or insects. I called my wife. At the end of the corridor the creature suddenly stopped in front of a door. "This is the headmistress's office, and she is already waiting for you", the monster said and then disappeared. When I knocked at the door, I heard a friendly voice saying, "Come in, please!" When I entered, I saw a lady ghost with long white hair and green eyes. She looked very pretty. I took my mobile phone. "I'm Haunty, the new teacher", I introduced myself *(ich stellte mich vor)*. "Oh, nice to meet you! Sit down, please! Have you got any teaching experience *(Erfahrung)*?" she asked.

"Yes, of course. Last year I worked at the school for magic in Canterbury."

"I see, then you know the basic rules you have to teach to our students. I'll show you your classroom", the headmistress said.

(In the classroom)

Haunty: Good morning, children! I'm Haunty, your teacher for this year. I'm hungry. I'm going to teach you everything you must know.
Ghost 1: Will we learn how to scare people?
Haunty: Of course, you will. Any further questions?
Ghost 2: Will we learn how to rattle chains?
Haunty: Not this year, that's in year two.
Ghost 3: I want to learn how to take my head off.
Haunty: Oh, that is easy. Wait a minute! I'll show you.

(Haunty says: "Abracadabra, head is off", and holds his head in his hands.

Ghost 3: Wow! Great! Let me try! Abracadabra, head is gone!
Haunty: No, don't say it!

But it was too late. The ghost's head was gone.
All the other ghosts laughed.

36 Put the sentences into the correct order and write the numbers (1–12). – *Bringe die Sätze in die richtige Reihenfolge und schreibe die Nummern 1–12 in die Kästchen.*

☐ Then we went upstairs and finally came to a long corridor.

☐ I'll show you your classroom.

☐ The ghost's head was gone.

☐ Have you got any teaching experience?

☐ Will we learn how to scare people?

☐ There were spiderwebs everywhere.

☐ Last year I worked at the school for magic in Canterbury.

☐ Wait a minute! I'll show you!

☐ Today was my first day at the new school.

☐ I'm not afraid of spiders or insects.

☐ Will we learn how to rattle chains?

37 Tick true or false. – *Kreuze richtig oder falsch an.*

		True	False
1	The ghost school was an old hotel.	☐	☐
2	It was high up on a mountain.	☐	☐
3	Haunty could not fly, so he had to walk.	☐	☐
4	A gigantic creature with three heads opened the door.	☐	☐
5	There were pictures of kings and queens on the wall.	☐	☐
6	Haunty was not afraid of spiders.	☐	☐
7	The headmistress had long white hair and blue eyes.	☐	☐
8	Haunty had worked at the school for magic in Canterbury.	☐	☐
9	Ghost 3 wants to learn how to rattle chains.	☐	☐
10	Ghost 2 wants to learn how to scare people.	☐	☐
11	The little ghost's head was gone.	☐	☐
12	The ghosts laughed.	☐	☐

READING

38 Answer the questions – *Beantworte die Fragen.*

1 Where is the ghost school?
___

2 Who opened the door?
___

3 Was Haunty afraid of spiders?
___

4 What did the headmistress look like?
___

5 Did Haunty have any teaching experience?
___

6 What did Ghost 1 want to learn?
___

7 What did Ghost 2 want to learn?
___

8 What did Ghost 3 want to learn?
___

9 What happened to Ghost 3?
___

10 How did Ghost 3 feel in the end?
___

My new pet

39 Read the text about Tim's new pet and tick the correct sentences. – *Lies den Text über Tims neues Haustier und kreuze die richtigen Sätze an.*

One day last summer I went to the park. I wanted to play football with my friends. When I arrived, nobody was there, so I sat down in the grass and waited. Suddenly I heard something above me. I looked up and couldn't believe my eyes. There seemed to be a monkey in the tree. "But this isn't possible! There are no monkeys in Austria!" I thought. But then the animal suddenly laughed and started throwing nuts at me. I stood up and went closer to the tree. It was definitely a monkey and it looked really cute. I tried to call the animal, but it did not come any closer.

After some time, my friends came. "You won't believe what I have just seen!" I said excitedly. "Follow me!" When they saw the monkey, they were really surprised. "Do you think it escaped *(entkam)* from a zoo?" Paul asked. "I don't know, but there is a circus in town, maybe we should ask them if they are missing a monkey", Patrick suggested *(schlug vor)*.

So I decided to go to the circus, and my friends stayed with the monkey. When I got there, I told the director of the circus *(Zirkusdirektor)* everything.

"Oh, I know which monkey you mean. Its name's Nelson, it is a very naughty *(schlimm)* animal. It doesn't know any tricks. I don't want it back, it is useless. You can keep it if you like," the man said. "But how can we catch Nelson?" I asked.

"Its favourite food are bananas. Give it one and it will be your friend forever."

The director of the circus was right, and now I have got a new pet.

1	I wanted to go swimming with my friends.	☐
2	The animal started throwing nuts at me.	☐
3	The monkey came closer.	☐
4	When they saw the monkey, they were really surprised.	☐
5	Paul thinks that Nelson escaped from a zoo.	☐
6	Tim told the director of the circus the whole story.	☐
7	The monkey's name is Jacky.	☐
8	The director of the circus wanted the monkey back.	☐
9	Nelson's favourite food are bananas.	☐
10	Now Tim has got a new pet.	☐

READING

40 Answer the questions. – *Beantworte die Fragen.*

1 Where did Tim go to?

2 What did he want to do there?

3 What did Tim suddenly hear?

4 Why couldn't he believe his eyes?

5 What did the animal suddenly do?

6 What is the monkey's name?

7 What did the director of the circus tell the boy about the monkey?

8 Why did he not want it back?

9 How did they catch the monkey?

10 Where does Nelson live now?

Holidays

41 Read the text and tick the correct sentences. – *Lies den Text und kreuze die richtigen Sätze an.*

Dear David,

I hope you are doing well back home. I'm in California. Everything is fine and I am having a great time. The weather is beautiful, and I go swimming every day. The sea is a bit cold, but the hotel I am staying has a great swimming pool. I spend most of my time there.

We have been *(sind gewesen)* to many interesting places. I like Los Angeles and Hollywood best. Guess what! I met Johnny Depp and he gave me his autograph *(Autogramm)*! I was so happy! He is really nice and looks even better than in his movies. I even took a selfie with him. I will show it to you when I'm back.

The food is delicious. I love Mexican food, especially the spicy dishes *(scharfe Gerichte)*.

My English has improved enormously, I have got a real American accent now.

Yesterday I met a very nice girl at the pool. She is staying at the same hotel. Her name is Susan and she comes from England.

I asked her if she wanted to go shopping with me and she said yes!!!

We also exchanged phone numbers, so I think we'll keep in touch.

I hope you are having a great time, too. Have fun and see you soon!

Tobias

1	A	Tobias is back home.	☐
	B	Tobias is in Florida.	☐
	C	Tobias is in California.	☐

2	A	He goes swimming every day.	☐
	B	He goes shopping every day.	☐
	C	He goes sightseeing every day.	☐

3	A	Tobias spends most of his time at the sea.	☐
	B	Tobias spends most of his time in his room.	☐
	C	Tobias spends most of his time at the pool.	☐

4	A	He has been to San Francisco.	☐
	B	He has been to Los Angeles.	☐
	C	He has been to New York.	☐

Bitte umblättern!

5
A	He met Johnny Depp.	☐
B	He didn't meet Johnny Depp.	☐
C	His sister met Johnny Depp.	☐

6
A	He took a selfie with Spiderman.	☐
B	He took a selfie with the Queen.	☐
C	He took a selfie with Johnny Depp.	☐

7
A	Tobias loves Italian food.	☐
B	Tobias loves fast food.	☐
C	Tobias loves Mexican food.	☐

8
A	Tobias met a girl from England.	☐
B	Tobias met a girl from Spain.	☐
C	Tobias met a girl from Germany.	☐

9
A	They went hiking.	☐
B	They went to the cinema.	☐
C	They went shopping.	☐

10
A	They exchanged phone numbers.	☐
B	They exchanged email addresses.	☐
C	They didn't exchange anything.	☐

I exchange phone numbers with nice persons, too!

42 Answer the questions. – *Beantworte die Fragen.*

1 Where does Tobias spend his holidays?
_____

2 Who does he write an email to?
_____

3 What is the weather like?
_____

4 Which places does he like best?
_____

5 Which famous person did he meet?
_____

6 What did he get from Johnny Depp?
_____

7 Has his English improved?
_____

8 What is the name of the girl from England?
_____

WRITING – SCHREIBÜBUNGEN

Last summer

43 Write a text about what you did last summer. Write about 80 words. – *Schreibe einen Text darüber, was du letzten Sommer getan hast. Schreibe etwa 80 Wörter.*

Write about:
- what you did
- if you went on holiday
- who you spent time with
- what you liked/didn't like

TIPP

Achte darauf, dass du in der Mitvergangenheit schreibst! Verwende auch folgende *linking words*, um deine Geschichte interessanter zu gestalten:
but, then, first, next, suddenly, later …

Dialogue about holidays

44 Write a dialogue between a boy and a girl talking about their holidays. Write about 100 words. – *Schreibe einen Dialog zwischen einem Jungen und einem Mädchen, die über ihren Urlaub plaudern. Schreibe etwa 100 Wörter.*

Start like this:

> A: *Hi, nice to see you again! You look so tanned* (**gebräunt**). *Where did you spend your holidays?*
> B: *I went to Spain …*

TIPP: Vergiss nicht darauf, dass sich die beiden höflich begrüßen und verabschieden. Achte auf die Fragebildung!

2 WRITING

45 A burglary

Someone broke into your house/flat and stole an expensive painting. An inspector is coming to your house to ask you some questions. Write about 130 words. – *Jemand ist in dein Haus / deine Wohnung eingebrochen und hat ein teures Bild gestohlen. Ein Polizist kommt zu dir nach Hause und stellt dir Fragen zum Einbruch. Schreibe etwa 130 Wörter.*

You can start like this:

> Inspector: Good evening! I'm Inspector Columbus. Can you tell me what happened?
> You: Yes, of course. Someone stole a very expensive painting.

TIPP: Versuche das gestohlene Bild so genau wie möglich zu beschreiben. Lass deiner Fantasie freien Lauf!

A terrible morning

46 Look at the pictures and write a story. Write about 150 words. Find a good title. Use the past tense. – *Schau dir die Bilder an und schreibe eine Bildergeschichte dazu. Schreibe etwa 150 Wörter. Finde auch einen passenden Titel für deine Geschichte. Schreibe in der Mitvergangenheit.*

You can start like this:

> Anna was lying in bed. She was having a really nice dream. Suddenly her alarm clock went off …

Bitte umblättern!

TIPP: Achte darauf, dass du in der Mitvergangenheit erzählst. Baue direkte Reden ein. Überlege dir einen passenden Titel erst, wenn du mit deiner Geschichte fertig bist.

Halloween

47 Here is the beginning of a Halloween story. Continue the story! Write about 120 words. Use the past tense. – *Hier ist der Beginn einer Halloween-Geschichte. Setze die Geschichte fort. Schreibe etwa 120 Wörter. Schreibe in der Mitvergangenheit.*

> Last Halloween I decided to have a party at home. I invited all my best friends, decorated the house and baked some really disgusting cookies …

TIPP: Schreibe eine spannende Geschichte und baue **direkte Reden** ein. Du kannst entweder ein reales Erlebnis beschreiben oder deiner Fantasie freien Lauf lassen. Schreibe in der **Mitvergangenheit**.

Description of a fantasy animal

48 Describe the Gruffollump from Atlantis. Write about 80 words. Use the past tense. – *Beschreibe den Gruffollump von Atlantis. Schreibe etwa 80 Wörter. Schreibe in der Mitvergangenheit.*

You should:
- describe the animal of Atlantis
- write about what it ate, where it lived
- write if you think it was dangerous …

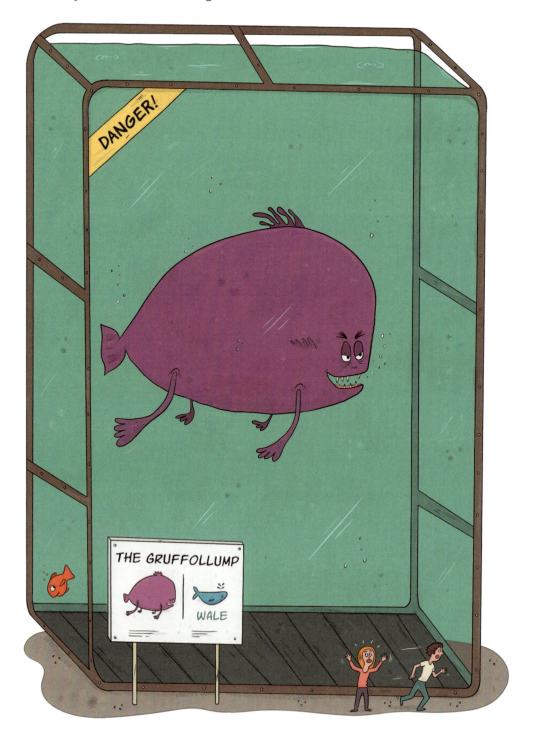

TIPP: Beschreibe zuerst das Bild. Du kannst aber auch **Dinge erfinden**. Überlege dir zusätzlich, ob dieses Tier gefährlich für den Menschen war, was es am liebsten aß, etc.
Schreibe in der **Mitvergangenheit**.

Description of your favourite fantasy animal

49 Write a text about your favourite fantasy animal. Write about 80 words. – *Schreibe einen Text über dein Lieblingsfantasietier. Schreibe ca. 80 Wörter.*

You can start like this:

> My favourite fantasy animal is a speaking elephant. It is smaller than a cat.

TIPP

Denke daran, dieses Tier gibt es nicht wirklich! Du kannst deiner Fantasie freien Lauf lassen.
Erwähne auch, warum es dein Lieblingsfantasietier ist. Welche Fähigkeiten/Eigenschaften machen es für dich so besonders?

Explaining the way

50 Look at the map and describe the way from the station to the football stadium and then to the cinema. Write a dialogue. Write about 100 words. – *Schau auf den Stadtplan und beschreibe den Weg vom Bahnhof zum Fußballstadion und dann zum Kino. Schreibe einen Dialog. Schreibe etwa 100 Wörter.*

You can start like this:

> A: Excuse me, can you tell me where the stadium and the cinema are?
> B: Yes, of course. First turn right. …

Bitte umblättern!

TIPP: Versuche die Wegbeschreibung so verständlich wie möglich zu gestalten. Beschreibe den **direkten Weg** und keine Umwege!

At a youth camp

51 Imagine you are at a youth camp and write an email to your parents. Write about 180 words. – *Stell dir vor, du bist in einem Ferienlager und schreibst eine E-Mail an deine Eltern. Schreibe etwa 180 Wörter.*

You should describe:
- what the camp is like
- where you are
- how you like it there
- what you can do there
- the rules at your camp
- what you did yesterday
- what you are going to do the next few days
- what you like/don't like

TIPP

Falls du wirklich schon einmal auf einem Ferienlager warst, kannst du natürlich dieses beschreiben. Wenn du eine E-Mail schreibst, beginne mit **Dear (Mum and Dad)**, und sage dann etwas Persönliches. Ende deine E-Mail mit **Yours, (your first name)**.

Party

52 You want to celebrate a fancy-dress party with all your friends. So you decide to write an invitation. Write about 80 words. – *Du möchtest eine Faschingsparty mit allen deinen Freundinnen / Freunden feiern. Daher beschließt du, eine Einladung zu schreiben. Schreibe etwa 80 Wörter.*

You should tell:
- what you are celebrating
- what costumes you expect
- when and where the party is

TIPP: Gestalte deine Einladung ansprechend, indem du etwas Nettes zeichnest.

From outer space

53 Look at the picture and write a science fiction story! Write about 140 words. Find a good title. Use the past tense. – *Schau dir das Bild an und schreibe eine Fantasiegeschichte. Schreibe etwa 140 Wörter. Finde einen passenden Titel. Schreibe in der Mitvergangenheit.*

You can start like this:

> One day, Peter was on his way to school. Suddenly he heard a strange noise. When he looked up at the sky, he suddenly saw ...

Bitte umblättern!

TIPP: Schreibe eine spannende Geschichte und verwende das Bild als Ausgangspunkt für deine Erzählung. Lasse deiner Fantasie freien Lauf. Baue auch **direkte Reden** ein und schreibe in der **Mitvergangenheit**.

At a restaurant

54 Write a dialogue at a restaurant. Use the following menu. Write about 100 words. – *Schreibe einen Dialog, der in einem Restaurant stattfindet. Verwende die abgebildete Speisekarte. Schreibe etwa 100 Wörter.*

You can start like this:

> Waiter: A table for two, madam?
> Woman: Yes, please.
> Man: Could we have the menu, please?
> Waiter: Certainly, sir. Are you ready to order no?

MENU
···Restaurant···

STARTERS:
- Tuna Salad
- Mozarella with tomatoes
- Onion Soup

MAIN COURSES:
- Veal with potatoes and salad
- Lasagne
- Fish and Chips
- Roastbeef with Yorkshire Pudding

DESSERTS:
- Chocolate ice cream
- Cheesecake
- Fruit salad

TIPP

Suche dir ein Gericht von der Speisekarte aus. Du kannst natürlich auch Getränke bestellen.

A ghost story

55 Look at the pictures and write a story. Use the phrases from the box. Write about 160 words. Use the past tense. – *Schau dir die Bilder an und schreibe eine Geschichte. Verwende die Phrasen aus der Box. Schreibe etwa 160 Wörter. Schreibe in der Mitvergangenheit.*

> Haunty was a young ghost …
> One night he wanted to …
> He knocked at the window …
> The girl laughed …
> Then Haunty …
> In the end, the ghost and the girl …

  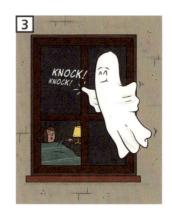

TIPP: Versuche zuerst die Bilder in deine Geschichte einzubauen, du kannst aber auch etwas **dazuerfinden**! Gib dem Mädchen einen **Namen**. Schreibe in der **Mitvergangenheit**.

Your house

56 Look at the plan of the house and describe what you see in each room. Write about 150 words. – *Schau auf den Plan des Hauses und beschreibe, was du in jedem Raum siehst. Schreibe etwa 150 Wörter.*

You can start like this:

> *Today I am going to describe my house. On the ground floor there is the living room ...*

TIPP: Versuche die Räume so genau wie möglich zu beschreiben. Schreibe in der Gegenwart.

WRITING 2

My dream house

57 Describe your dream house. Write about 60 words. – *Beschreibe dein Traumhaus. Schreibe etwa 60 Wörter*

You can start like this:

> My dream house is close to the beach. It is very big and white. ...

TIPP: Überlege dir, wie dein Traumhaus aussehen soll. Welche **Räume** hättest du gerne in deinem Haus? Wie sieht die **Umgebung** aus (**Garten** etc.). Lass deiner Fantasie freien Lauf!

What a pity!

Hi guys, no swimming for four weeks. Do you want to know why? I broke my legs when I jumped into the lake last week. Unfortunately, the water wasn't deep enough, so I hit the ground. Both my legs are in plaster now, so I can't walk. I have to stay in bed for another three weeks, which means that I can't go to Greece. My parents have already cancelled the flight. I'm sooooo frustrated!!!!

58 Read the message above and imagine that the writer is a friend of yours. Write a message back. Write about 80 words. – *Lies die Nachricht oben und stelle dir vor, die Schreiberin / der Schreiber der Nachricht ist eine Freundin / ein Freund von dir. Schreibe ihr / ihm zurück. Schreibe etwa 80 Wörter.*

Include the following points:
- Say that you feel sorry for her/him.
- Try to make her/him feel better.
- Tell her/him something funny, interesting.
- Promise to visit her/him soon.

TIPP

Versetze dich in die Lage deiner Freundin / deines Freundes und versuche, so viel **Mitgefühl** wie möglich zu zeigen.

Families

59 You have got a new pen friend who wants to visit you. You write her/him an email where you describe your family. Write about 130 words. – *Du hast eine neue Brieffreundin/einen neuen Brieffreund, die/der dich besuchen möchte. Du schreibst ihr/ihm eine E-Mail, in der du deine Familie beschreibst. Schreibe etwa 130 Wörter.*

You can start like this:

> Hi ...,
> How are you? I am really looking forward to seeing you. To make you feel more comfortable, I want to introduce **(vorstellen)** my family to you. ...

Your favourite star

60 Describe the life and family of your favourite star. Write about 80 words. –
Beschreibe das Leben und die Familie deines Lieblingsstars. Schreibe ca. 80 Wörter.

You can start like this:

> My favourite star is a football player. His name is …

TIPP

Du kannst eine Sportlerin/einen Sportler, eine Sängerin/einen Sänger oder eine Schauspielerin/einen Schauspieler wählen. Recherchiere im Internet, wenn du zusätzliche Informationen benötigst.
Erwähne auch kurz, warum du diese Person so bewunderst.

The weather

61 Write a dialogue between you and a friend where you talk about your holidays. Also talk about the weather. Write about 100 words. – *Schreibe einen Dialog zwischen dir und deiner Freundin / deinem Freund, worin du über deinen Urlaub plauderst. Sprich auch über das Wetter. Schreibe etwa 100 Wörter.*

You can start like this:

> A: Hi! How are you? I haven't seen you for ages **(seit Ewigkeiten)**.
> B: I spent the last month in Great Britain.
> A: Oh really? Did you have a good time? What was the weather like?
> B: Well, most of the time it was okay. ...

TIPP: Versuche auch über das **Wetter** zu schreiben. Du kannst einen **Urlaub** beschreiben, den du wirklich erlebt hast, oder etwas erfinden. Achte darauf, deine Freundin/deinen Freund am Beginn zu **begrüßen** und dich am Schluss zu **verabschieden**.

The weather forecast for Austria

62 Take a look at the map of Austria and write a report for the weatherman. Write about 90 words. – *Schau auf die Österreichkarte und schreibe den Wetterbericht für den Präsentator der Wetternachrichten. Schreibe etwa 90 Wörter.*

You can start like this:

> R: Good evening! This is the weather report for tomorrow. In the northeast of Austria the good weather continues, temperatures will rise to 30 degrees. ...

TIPP: Schau dir die Wetterkarte genau an und beschreibe, was du darauf siehst. Orientiere dich an den **Himmelsrichtungen** (Norden – Osten – Süden – Westen).

Tomorrow's weather

63 Write a text about tomorrow's weather where you live. Write about 40 words. – *Schreibe einen Wetterbericht über das morgige Wetter in deinem Heimatort. Schreibe etwa 40 Wörter.*

Start like this:

> Tomorrow there will be …

TIPP: Verwende die *will-future*, da du dir ja nicht sicher sein kannst, wie das Wetter wirklich sein wird.

Ancient Egypt

64 Here is the beginning of a story. Continue the story. Find a good title for your story. Write about 200 words. Use the past tense. – *Hier ist der Beginn einer Geschichte. Setze die Geschichte fort. Finde einen passenden Titel für deine Geschichte. Schreibe etwa 200 Wörter. Schreibe in der Mitvergangenheit.*

Jacob was on holiday in Egypt. It was a very hot day and he and his family stayed at the pool. There were no other kids and the boy soon felt bored. So he decided to explore *(erkunden)* the garden of the hotel. After some time he came to a little house. It looked very old and shabby *(heruntergekommen)*. Jacob became curious and opened the door. It was dark inside and there was a strange smell. …

TIPP: Achte darauf, dass deine Geschichte in **Ägypten** spielt, das heißt, du kannst **Mumien** oder **Pharaonen** einbauen. Deine Geschichte soll **spannend** und **geheimnisvoll** wirken. Baue **direkte Reden** ein. Schreibe in der **Mitvergangenheit** und überlege dir den **Titel** erst, wenn du mit deiner Geschichte fertig bist.

Adventure story

65 Look at the picture and write an adventure story. Find a good title! Write about 220 words. Use the past tense. – *Schau dir das Bild an und schreibe eine Abenteuergeschichte. Finde einen passenden Titel. Schreibe etwa 220 Wörter. Schreibe in der Mitvergangenheit.*

___

TIPP

Du kannst die **Abenteuergeschichte** entweder aus der **Perspektive** der Erzählerin/des Erzählers schildern oder aus der Sicht eines der beiden Kinder im Zelt.
Achte darauf, dass deine Geschichte realistisch bleibt. Es soll keine Fantasiegeschichte werden!
Gib den Personen **Namen**, baue **direkte Reden** ein. Schreibe in der **Mitvergangenheit** und vergiss nicht auf den **Titel**.

Sports

66 Write a dialogue where two children talk about their favourite sport. Write about 100 words. – *Schreibe einen Dialog, in dem sich zwei Kinder über ihren Lieblingssport unterhalten. Schreibe etwa 100 Wörter.*

You can start like this:

> A: Hi! How are you?
> B: I'm fine. I'm on my way to my second tennis lesson.
> A: Really? I didn't know that you were into tennis. When did you start? ...

TIPP

Erwähne in deinem Dialog, **seit wann** du diese Sportart ausübst, wie **oft** du trainierst, **warum** du diesen Sport magst, **ob du gut darin bist**, ob du bereits an **Wettkämpfen** teilgenommen hast ... Du kannst natürlich auch etwas erfinden. Achte darauf, dass du deine Freundin/deinen Freund **begrüßt** und **verabschiedest**.

Linda's favourite sport

67 Take a look at Linda and write about her favourite sport. Write about 60 words.

– *Schau dir das Bild von Linda an und schreibe über ihren Lieblingssport. Schreibe etwa 60 Wörter.*

You can start like this:

> *This is Linda. Her favourite sport is tennis. …*

TIPP

Schreibe, **wann** und **wie oft** Linda diese Sportart ausübt, **seit wann** sie Tennis spielt …

Paul's favourite sport

68 Take a look at Paul and write about his favourite sport. Write about 60 words. – *Schau dir das Bild von Paul an und schreibe über seinen Lieblingssport. Schreibe etwa 60 Wörter.*

You can start like this:

> This is Paul. His favourite sport is surfing. ...

TIPP: Schreibe, **wann** und **wie oft** Paul diese Sportart ausübt, **seit wann** er sie ausübt …

Pets

69 Imagine you have got a new pet. Write a diary entry where you describe your first time with your pet. Write about 110 words. – *Stell dir vor, du hast ein neues Haustier bekommen. Schreibe eine Tagebucheintragung, in der du die erste Zeit mit deinem Haustier beschreibst. Schreibe etwa 110 Wörter.*

You can start like this:

> Dear Diary,
> I have great news for you. Three days ago, I got a new pet. Her name is ... and she is a ...

TIPP

Nenne den **Namen deines Haustieres**, schreibe, um **welches Tier** es sich handelt. Beschreibe, welche **Eigenschaften** und **Gewohnheiten** dein Tier hat. Erzähle auch, wie du dich mit deinem Haustier **beschäftigst**. Erwähne, wie oft du es **fütterst**. …

Wenn du kein Haustier hast, dann kannst du natürlich auch das einer Freundin / eines Freundes beschreiben beziehungsweise ein Tier, welches du gerne als Haustier hättest.

Dialogue about your pet

70 Write a dialogue where a boy and a girl talk about their pets. Write about 90 words. – *Schreibe einen Dialog, in welchem sich ein Junge und ein Mädchen über ihre Haustiere unterhalten. Schreibe etwa 90 Wörter.*

You can start like this:

> Cathy: Hi Matthew! Is this your dog?
> Matthew: Hi Cathy! Yes, her name is Nancy. ...

TIPP: Wenn du ein eigenes Haustier hast, kannst du es in deinen Dialog einbauen. Ansonsten lass deiner Fantasie freien Lauf!

Animals

71 Take a look at these four animals and compare them. Which one is cooler, more beautiful, stronger, heavier, more intelligent, faster, quicker, smaller …? Write about 70 words. – *Schau dir die Bilder zu den vier Tieren an und vergleiche sie. Welches ist cooler, hübscher, stärker, schwerer, intelligenter, schneller, beweglicher, kleiner …? Schreibe etwa 70 Wörter.*

You can start like this:

Minny, the mouse, is smaller than Carlo, the cat.

TIPP

Versuche so viele **Unterschiede** bzw. **Gemeinsamkeiten** zwischen den Tieren zu finden wie möglich. Du kannst den Tieren auch **Namen** geben.

Rules

72 Write down the rules for your birthday party. Write about 60 words. – *Schreibe die Regeln für deine Geburtstagsparty auf. Schreibe ca. 60 Wörter.*

You can use the following words:

| must • must not • should • should not • have to • don't have to … |

TIPP Überlege, welche Regeln für dich bei deiner Party gelten würden.

Schools

73 Write a text about the rules at your school. Write down at least ten rules. – *Schreibe einen Text über die Regeln in deiner Schule. Schreibe mindestens 10 Regeln auf.*

You can use the following words:

| must • must not • should • should not • have to • don't have to … |

TIPP Überlege, welche Regeln es an deiner Schule gibt (im **Klassenzimmer**, im **Pausenhof**, auf dem **Gang** …).

Your dream school

74 Describe your dream school. Write about 90 words. – *Beschreibe deine Traumschule. Schreibe etwa 90 Wörter.*

You can start like this:

> At my dream school, there shouldn't be any tests. …

TIPP Überlege, wie deine Traumschule aussehen könnte. Beschreibe nicht nur das **Gebäude** und die **Klassenzimmer**, sondern auch, welche **Regeln** du gerne hättest. Beschreibe auch, wie du dir deine **Traumlehrerin** / deinen **Traumlehrer** vorstellst.

Holidays

75 Write an email to your friend and tell her/him about your last day at school. Write about 150 words. – *Schreibe eine E-Mail an deine Freundin / deinen Freund und erzähle ihr / ihm von deinem letzten Schultag. Schreibe etwa 150 Wörter.*

You can start like this:

> Hi ...,
> I'm so happy! Today was my last day of school.

TIPP Erwähne in deiner E-Mail auch, welche Pläne du für den Sommer hast. Wenn du etwas schon geplant hast oder sicher weißt, verwende die ***going to*-future**.

Plans for next school year

76 Write about the plans for you next school year. Write about 80 words. – *Schreibe über deine Pläne für nächstes Schuljahr. Schreibe ca. 80 Wörter.*

You can start like this:

> Next year I will always listen to the teacher. ...

TIPP

Überlege, was du im nächsten Schuljahr besser machen könntest. Da es sich um **gute Vorsätze** handelt, verwende die *will-future*.

How embarrassing!

77 Look at the pictures and write a story! Use the past tense! Write about 150 words! Use the following words for your story – *Schau dir die Bilder an und schreibe eine Geschichte dazu. Schreibe in der Mitvergangenheit! Schreibe ca. 150 Wörter. Verwende folgende Wörter für deine Geschichte:*

public swimming pool *(Freibad)* • diving platform *(Sprungturm)* • diving board *(Sprungbrett)*

TIPP

Da es sich um ein **peinliches Erlebnis** handelt, beschreibe auch die **Gefühle** der Personen.
Konzentriere dich zuerst auf die Bilder, du kannst deine Erzählung auch etwas ausschmücken.
Gib den beiden Jungen **Namen** und baue auch **direkte Reden** ein.

DURCHSTARTEN LERNHILFEN –
FÜR GUTE NOTEN UND EIN ENTSPANNTES FAMILIENLEBEN!

VERITAS hat sich mit der (Weiter-)Entwicklung der Durchstarten-Lernhilfen das Ziel gesetzt, allen SchülerInnen in Österreich – von der Volksschule bis zur Matura – **gute Noten** und **nachhaltigen Lernerfolg** zu ermöglichen und dadurch für weniger Stress in der Familie und der Schule zu sorgen.

Somit tragen die Durchstarten-Lernhilfen auch zu einem **entspannten Familienleben** bei.

ÖSTERREICHISCHER LEHRPLAN

Unsere Leitlinien:

- Die Durchstarten-Lernhilfen werden **von erfahrenen PädagogInnen/LehrerInnen entwickelt**.
- Wir orientieren uns an den aktuellen formalen **Anforderungen des österreichischen Lehrplans** und unterstützen dadurch die **bildungsrelevanten Ziele Österreichs**.
- Die Lernhilfen können **unabhängig vom jeweils verwendeten Schulbuch** eingesetzt werden.
- Bei der Produktentwicklung legen wir den Fokus auf die Anforderungen und Wünsche der Verwendergruppen – also **SchülerInnen, Eltern und LehrerInnen**.
- Digitale Inhalte und Funktionen, wie zum Beispiel das Anhören von Hörverständnisübungen am Smartphone, werden dort eingesetzt, wo sie das **Lernen sinnvoll unterstützen**.
- **Keine Übung kommt zweimal vor.**

So stiften wir großen Kundennutzen für SchülerInnen, LehrerInnen und Eltern:

SchülerInnen
mehr Lernerfolg/bessere Noten bei geringerem zeitlichem Übungsaufwand und somit mehr Freizeit und weniger Probleme mit Eltern und/oder LehrerInnen

LehrerInnen
Sicherheit, immer das passende lehrwerksunabhängige, aber lehrplankonforme Übungsmaterial zu haben (z. B. für die **Differenzierung**)

Eltern
entspanntes Familienleben (kein Schul-/Notenstress)

Mehr Infos unter: www.durchstarten.at

Bibliografische Information Der Deutschen Bibliothek
Die Deutsche Bibliothek verzeichnet diese Publikation in der Deutschen Nationalbibliografie;
detaillierte bibliografische Daten sind im Internet über http://dnb.ddb.de abrufbar.

© VERITAS-VERLAG, Linz. Alle Rechte vorbehalten.
Das Werk und seine Teile sind urheberrechtlich geschützt. Jede Nutzung in anderen als den gesetzlich
zugelassenen Fällen bedarf der vorherigen schriftlichen Einwilligung des Verlages.

1. Auflage (2020) – Entspricht der Rechtschreibreform 2006.

Gedruckt auf umweltfreundlich hergestelltem Papier
AutorInnen: Nicole Eisinger-Müllner, Julie Eiwen, Franz Zach
Lektorat: Klaus Kopinitsch
Bildredaktion: Raffaela Schuster
Umschlaggestaltung und Layout: Kathrin Schager
Herstellung: Sandra Reinhardt
Illustrationen: Sven Aring, Paderborn
Satz: FACTORY punkt Werbeagentur GmbH, Traun
Umschlagfotos: stock.adobe.com/Dima

Der Verlag hat sich bemüht, alle Rechtsinhaber ausfindig zu machen. Sollten trotzdem Urheberrechte verletzt
worden sein, wird der Verlag nach Anmeldung berechtigter Ansprüche diese entgelten. Soweit Personen
fotografisch abgebildet sind und ihnen Namen, Dialoge und Ähnliches zugeordnet sind, dient dies nur der
Veranschaulichung und dem besseren Verständnis des Inhaltes.

ISBN 978-3-7101-3781-5

Für weitere Informationen steht Ihnen gerne Ihre VERITAS-Kundenberatung zur Verfügung.
Rufen Sie einfach an, schicken Sie ein Fax oder ein E-Mail!
Tel. +43 732 776451 2280, Fax: +43 732 776451 2239
E-Mail: kundenberatung@veritas.at
Besuchen Sie uns auf unserer Website www.veritas.at